Gay and Lesbian Parents

THE CHANGING FACE OF MODERN FAMILIES

Adoptive Parents
Blended Families
Celebrity Families
Families Living with Mental & Physical Challenges
First-Generation Immigrant Families
Foster Families
Gay and Lesbian Parents
Grandparents Raising Kids
Growing Up in Religious Communities
Kids Growing Up Without a Home
Multiracial Families
Single Parents
Teen Parents
What Is a Family?

Gay and Lesbian Parents

Julianna Fields

Mason Crest Publishers, Inc.

MASON CREST PUBLISHERS INC.
370 Reed Road
Broomall, Pennsylvania 19008
(866)MCP-BOOK (toll free)
www.masoncrest.com

First Printing

9 8 7 6 5 4 3 2 1

ISBN 978-1-4222-1495-4
ISBN 978-1-4222-1490-9 (series)
Library of Congress Cataloging-in-Publication Data
Fields, Julianna.

Produced by Harding House Publishing Service, Inc. www.hardinghousepages.com
Interior Design by MK Bassett-Harvey.
Cover design by Asya Blue www.asyablue.com.
Printed in The United States of America.

Photo Credits

Creative Commons Attribution Share-Alike: bobster855 13, Jonathunder 49, nerdcoregirl 10, 27, 30; United States White House: Souza, Pete 39

Contents

Introduction

The Gallup Poll has become synonymous with accurate statistics on what people really think, how they live, and what they do. Founded in 1935 by statistician Dr. George Gallup, the Gallup Organization continues to provide the world with unbiased research on who we really are.

From recent Gallup Polls, we can learn a great deal about the modern family. For example, a June 2007 Gallup Poll reported that Americans, on average, believe the ideal number of children for a family to have these days is 2.5. This includes 56 percent of Americans who think it is best to have a small family of one, two, or no children, and 34 percent who think it is ideal to have a larger family of three or more children; nine percent have no opinion. Another recent Gallup Poll found that when Americans were asked, "Do you think homosexual couples should or should not have the legal right to adopt a child," 49 percent of Americans said they should, and 48 percent said they shouldn't; 43 percent supported the legalization of gay marriage, while 57 percent did not. Yet another poll found that 34 percent of Americans feel a conflict between the demands of their professional life and their family life; 39 percent still believe that one parent should ideally stay home with the children while the other works.

Keep in mind that Gallup Polls do not tell us what is right or wrong. They don't report on what people should think—only on what they do think. And what is clear from Gallup Polls is that while the shape of families is changing in our modern world, the concept of family is still vital to our sense of who we are and how we interact with others. An indication of this is the 2008 Gallup poll that found that three out of four Americans reported that family values are important, while one in three said they are "extremely" important.

And how do Americans define "family values"? According to the same poll, here's what Americans say is their definition of a family: a strong unit where faith and morals, education and integrity play important roles within the structure of a committed relationship.

The books in the series demonstrate that strong family units come in all shapes and sizes. Those differences, however, do not change the faith, integrity, and commitment of the families who tell their stories within these books.

1 Homosexuality and Parenting

Terms to Understand

controversial: causing debates, arguments, and strong differences in opinion.
conservatives: people who are more likely to support traditional values and viewpoints and oppose change.
liberals: people who are more likely to support progress, reform, and a maximum of individual freedoms.
alternative: following non-traditional or unconventional methods or ideas; existing outside of the established ways of doing things.
peer group: a group of people, generally of the same age and social status who associate with each other and influence each other's ideas and behaviors.
sexual orientation: a person's sexual preference for those of the same, opposite , or both genders.
irrelevant: making no difference or having no connection to a subject or issue under discussion.

Thirty years ago in the United States about a half a million gay and lesbian parents were raising children. Today, those numbers have risen. About 10 million children are being raised in a gay or lesbian household.

So how are these kids doing?

Controversy

Homosexual partnerships are a ***controversial*** topic in twenty-first–century America, one that divides political parties and creates strong feelings, both for and against. It's no wonder, then, that homosexual families would come under close investigation.

Conservatives believe that the children growing up in families led by homosexual parents are more apt to struggle with a variety of issues, including self-esteem, sexual identity, economic stability, and mental health. Dr. James Dobson, founder of the conservative Christian group Focus on the Family, said in *Time* magazine in December 2008 that "the majority of more than 30 years of social-science evidence indicates that children do best on every measure of well-being when raised by their married mother and father." Newspaper columnist Leonard Pitts agreed, saying that "a growing body of research that tells us the child raised without his or her biological father is significantly more likely to live in poverty, do poorly in school, drop out altogether, become a teen parent, exhibit behavioral problems, smoke, drink, use drugs or wind up in jail."

Meanwhile, ***liberals*** insist that children are not harmed in these ***alternative*** families, and that in fact, there are advantages to having a gay or lesbian parent. "These kids tend to be more tolerant," said one teacher who has had in her class children from same-sex families. "They're kinder to the other kids. They're more respectful to adults and to each other."

And what does the research say? Most studies have found that outcomes for children of gay and lesbian parents are no better—and no worse!—than for other children, whether the measures

Terms to Understand

intentional: done on purpose; planned.

surrogacy: when a woman becomes pregnant on behalf of a couple who is unable or unwilling to become pregnant themselves, either though in vitro fertilization, using a donated egg and sperm, or through artificial insemination, using her own egg and donated sperm.

stigma: shame or disgrace; something that harms a person's reputation.

discrimination: when a person is treated differently because of some category to which that person belongs, rather than being judged as an individual.

prejudice: opinions or ideas about a person, group, or thing, formed before knowing much about him, her, or it.

Do you see a family in this picture? These women made a commitment to each other, and chose to adopt, raise and love two children. What are they, if not a family?

involve ***peer group*** relationships, self-esteem, behavioral difficulties, academic achievement, or warmth and quality of family relationships. In 67 studies presented by the American Psychological Association, children in homosexual-parent families turned out the same, for better or for worse, as children in heterosexual families. These studies found that the ***sexual orientation*** of a parent is ***irrelevant*** to the development of a child's mental health and the quality of a parent-child relationship.

Are Homosexual Two-Parent Families Different from Heterosexual Parents?

The answer to that question is often, "Yes." But the reason may not be one that occurs to most people.

Same-sex couples are like heterosexual couples: they can be poor or wealthy; black, brown, or white; educated or uneducated; well-adjusted or not. But same-sex parents all have one thing in common that sets them apart from some heterosexual parents: same-sex parents are ***intentional***.

This means that homosexual couples have to make an active decision to have children; it's not something that can happen to them accidentally. They will have to take definite steps to become parents, either through adoption or ***surrogacy***. Because these steps tend to cost money, same-sex–parent families are likely to be white and have higher incomes; they're often better educated; they're comfortable with their sexual orientation; and they have a stable relationship with each other.

Most of the research has been done on this kind of homosexual family. Children growing up in stable families with plenty of economic and educational resources tend to do well, regardless of their parents' sexual orientation.

What About One-Parent Families?

Most children with a homosexual parent aren't living in a two-parent home. Instead, their mother or father usually came out after they were born, breaking the biological family unit. According to U.S. Census figures, about 45 percent of homosexual parents in this situation are black or Latino with lower incomes than the families built by two homosexual partners. Homosexuality does not tend to be discussed as openly or accepted in minority communities, which often means that children with a homosexual parent may face ***stigma*** that causes them to experience shame and embarrassment.

WHY DO MINORITY GROUPS ON AVERAGE HAVE LOWER INCOMES THAN WHITES?
Because minority groups still face ***discrimination*** and ***prejudice*** in American society, they do not always have the same employment and educational opportunities that white Americans have. This in turn affects how much money minorities are able to make on average.

What Is a Family?

Ultimately, sociologists agree that more research needs to be done on same-sex parents. It's safe to say, though, that each family with homosexual-parents faces a unique set of challenges even as it experiences unique opportunities. That's the same with any family. No two sets of parents are exactly alike, and no blanket assumptions can be made about any family.

And what goes almost without saying, something that even the most conservative critics admit: children growing up with same-sex parents truly *are* growing up in a family. As one sixth-grade child of lesbian mothers said, "Family means the people who look out for me and treat me with love and respect. My family are the people who are in my life practically every day. . . . We all like to ride our bikes and go places together. Don't be ashamed of who your parents are."

Sociologists Judith Stacey and Timothy Biblarz published an analysis in 2001 in the *American Sociological Review* of twenty-one studies of children raised by homosexual parents and found that, overall, they were no more likely to suffer from psychological problems than kids raised in conventional homes. "We know that a parent's sexual orientation is not a significant factor [in mental health]," said Stacey. "A good parent is a good parent, . . . and parents who

These men chose to adopt a child. There are no accidental adoptions—the couple has to want a child badly enough to complete the long and involved adoption process.

get along and are consistent in their child-rearing . . . have better outcomes than those who don't."

"Love binds parents and children together, not gender," says sociologist Dr. Kyle Pruett.

HEADLINES

(From the *Pittsburgh Post-Gazette*, June 10, 2007, "What Happens to Kids Raised by Gay Parents?" by Mackenzie Carpenter)

Rebecca Meiksin, 22, is white, middle-class, college-educated, with plans to earn a graduate degree in public health.

Terrance McGeorge, 20, is black, grew up in [a low-income community], has a high school degree and works in an AmeriCorps service program at Beginning With Books.

Despite their differences, both of these young people have something in common with the new grandson of the vice president of the United States, who was born to Mary Cheney and her partner, Heather Poe, on May 23: They grew up in a family with a gay parent.

And both of them believe they have turned out just fine—in no small way because of how they were raised.

"My dad has been my best friend since I was a kid," said Mr. McGeorge, a tall, friendly young man who wants to pursue a career in theater and fashion. "He always encouraged me and was there for me, for whatever it was, graduations, performances, he was there, immediately."

Mr. McGeorge, like his father, is gay. That might provoke an "Aha!" moment for those who warn that children of gays are more likely to adopt their parents' lifestyle, but he says his father had nothing to do with it, except, possibly, providing DNA. . . .

Ms. Meiksin is heterosexual. . . . Asked if her lesbian mother encouraged her to follow in her footsteps, she rolls her eyes.

"I never felt any pressure to be gay," she said. "Although I did take my boyfriend to a gay pride parade once, which was a real trip for him."

Ms. Meiksin represents part of a first wave of babies intentionally conceived or adopted by gay parents in the 1980s as the gay pride movement took off. Mr. McGeorge, on the other hand, is part of a different group of children—many from minority and low-income communities—born of a heterosexual union that dissolved when one parent came out as gay. . . .

Mr. McGeorge says . . . that when his father first came out, he recalls, children in his Hill District neighborhood "cut me no slack whatsoever. They all knew about it. He looked different, acted different, and they made sure I knew it."

. . . One of the reasons for that is because of a high level of intolerance of homosexuality in the African-American community, Mr. McGeorge believes.

"Oh my God, I think maybe four or five times a week I'm getting called 'faggot,'" he said. "I can't go into a store to buy cigarettes without being told I'm a 'faggot' and I'm going to hell. I can't get on a bus without someone getting in my face. Sometimes the discrimination hurts, but I'm unapologetic for who I am. I won't apologize and I won't change for anyone. I've always just been myself."

On the other hand, Ms. Meiksin, born to a single lesbian mother in Squirrel Hill who moved in with a partner when Ms. Meiksin was 12, says she rarely felt any kind of discomfort growing up. . . . A graduate of Allderdice High School and Oberlin College, in Ohio, she says her life "always felt normal to me."

What Do You Think?

In what ways do you think Rebecca Meiksin and Terrence McGeorge are alike? In what ways do you think they are different? What do you think explains these differences?

2 Two Mothers

Terms to Understand

artificial insemination: the process of putting semen into a woman's vagina or uterus without sexual contact.
donor: a person who gives, or donates, something.
nurturers: those people who naturally tend to feed, protect, support, or encourage others.
stereotypes: oversimplified, formulaic images or opinions.
fundamentalist: one who strictly follows a set of basic beliefs or principles, especially a type of American protestant Christianity that believes the Bible is literally true, both historically and morally.
abhorrent: causing hatred or disgust.

A big orange cat sits grooming himself on the front stoop. Bright-colored letters on the window spell out W-E-L-C-O-M-E.

The tidy white house is one of eight others on a one-block section of the suburban street, and all the houses are as similar as their working-class occupants. They keep neat lawns, attend their kids' softball games, hold down blue-collar jobs that never pay quite enough.

The door opens to reveal the family inside: two parents, two children, a dog and another cat. And for the first time, a visitor to the house realizes there's something different about this house and its family.

It has two mothers.

Thirty-one-year-old Heather Howard gave birth to the family's three-year-old son, Harrison, and year-old daughter, Madeline; she got pregnant by

artificial insemination from the same unknown ***donor***. Her partner, Patsy Sloane, adopted both children in a second-parent process for such situations. The women have been together eleven years, and they've owned this little three-bedroom two-story house for seven of those years.

Sometimes, Harrison's friends ask, "Who's the mommy?"

Two voices always chime in response: "I am."

Patsy, who is forty-two, admits she felt jealous that Heather was the one to carry Maddy and Harry under her heart, that Heather was the one who could nurse the babies at her breast.

But like any two parents, Patsy and Heather have many overlapping roles in the family. Both are ***nurturers*** and caregivers, both cook great beef stew and goulash, both combat the constant onslaught of cat and dog fur with their heavy-duty Hoover Wind Tunnel. But Heather's the one who can change a tire in five minutes flat, while Patsy's more apt to be scrubbing Harry's jeans to get out the grass stains.

In those roles, they don't fit the ***stereotypes***, Patsy notes with a laugh: she's the "butch" one, with short, spiked hair, while Heather's more feminine, and her hair forms a soft frame around her face. Joking about themselves, the two women show just how

Terms to Understand

condone: to treat something as acceptable or forgivable.
in vitro conception: when an egg is fertilized with a sperm in a laboratory setting, outside the human body, usually to create an embryo to be implanted in a uterus.
homophobia: fear or hatred of gay men and lesbians.
diversity: having differences or variety.
transgendered: having the characteristics that go beyond one gender or gender norms.

Religion & Homosexuality

Most of the world's largest religions view homosexuality negatively. This can range from quietly discouraging homosexual activity, to explicitly forbidding same-sex sexual practices and actively opposing social acceptance of homosexuality. Some teach that homosexual orientation itself is sinful, while others say that only the sexual act is a sin. Some claim that homosexuality can be overcome through religious faith and practice. Conservative evangelical Christians in particular generally believe that homosexuality is sinful, and many believe that the political push for legalized same-sex marriages is a threat to American's moral values. "Of course God loves the homosexual," says one conservative Christian, "just as He loves the liar and the thief. But He hates homosexuality in the same way He hates lying and stealing. As Christians we are called to restore His kingdom on earth by fighting against any acceptance of sin, whether that be homosexuality or dishonesty."

comfortable they are with their situation—and their sexuality.

Not that their parents came to grips with it so easily. Heather's father, a ***fundamentalist*** minister, believed the Bible considered homosexuality to be a sin and its practitioners to be sinners. That his daughter "chose" to be gay was ***abhorrent*** to him. Her mother wasn't as

Meanwhile, other Christian denominations do not condemn homosexual acts as bad or evil, and there is a denomination of 40,000 members, the Metropolitan Community Church, that is committed to being open and affirming to homosexuals. The United Church of Christ also ***condones*** gay marriage and some parts of the Anglican and Lutheran churches allow for the blessing of gay unions. The United Church of Canada also allows same-sex marriage, and views sexual orientation as a gift from God. These Christians would say that religion's attitudes against homosexuality are based on cultural traditions rather than on what God wants. "God wants us to love each other," says one liberal Christian. "God wants us to honor each other, to treat each other with respect and integrity, to put others needs above our own. All that can be done within the context of a homosexual relationship equally as well as within a heterosexual one."

strict, but she knew better than to dispute her husband's authority about religious matters.

"She was very concerned to think I might never be able to have children," Heather says.

What Do You Think?

Do you believe homosexuality should be a religious issue? Why or why not? Why do you think people feel so strongly on both sides of the issue?

What Is PFLAG?

The PFLAG's website (community.pflag.org/Page.aspx?pid=194&srcid=-2) states:

Our Vision

We, the parents, families and friends of lesbian, gay, bisexual and transgender persons, celebrate diversity and envision a society that embraces everyone, including those of diverse sexual orientations and gender identities. Only with respect, dignity and equality for all will we reach our full potential as human beings, individually and collectively. PFLAG welcomes the participation and support of all who share in, and hope to realize this vision.

Our Mission

PFLAG promotes the health and well-being of gay, lesbian, bisexual and transgender persons, their families and friends through: support, to cope with an adverse society; education, to enlighten an ill-informed public; and advocacy, to end discrimination and to secure equal civil rights. Parents, Families and Friends of Lesbians and Gays provides opportunity for dialogue about sexual orientation and gender identity, and acts to create a society that is healthy and respectful of human diversity.

Patsy had been raised in a single-parent household that never talked about much of anything, particularly not the birds and the bees. If gayness was mentioned at all, it was with ridicule, the stuff of jokes and insults.

Always a tomboy by nature, Patsy found herself more and more the butt of those cruel jokes at school. By then, in her early teens, she had already realized she wasn't drawn to boys (although she did later date some) – but she didn't dare tell anybody about the crushes she had on various girls.

One day she stumbled on a poster for a group called PFLAG (Parents, Families and Friends of Lesbians and Gays), inviting teenagers questioning their orientation to a meeting. Late after school, when the hall was empty, she quickly jotted down the time and place.

HEADLINES

(From "ONE MOTHER'S VOICE: PFLAG Cofounder Recalls Group's Beginnings," by Tom Owens, Tolerance.org, July 14, 2005.)

Jeanne Manford needs few words to make the most complex questions simple. "I loved him," she said of her son, Morty Manford. "He was my son."

That love and pride inspired Manford to co-found the internationally-known support group Parents, Families and Friends of Lesbians and Gays (PFLAG) in 1972.

"Of course, I knew Morty was gay," Manford explained. "He didn't want to tell me. I told him that I loved him, and nothing else mattered. At first, there was a little tension there. He didn't believe I was that accepting. But I was."

In 1972, Morty was punched, kicked and thrown down an escalator during a gay rights protest at the New York City Hilton Hotel. Manford and her husband watched the attacks on the evening TV news, outraged that police officers appeared to ignore the assault.

Manford's next steps erased any doubt her son may have had about her loyalty and acceptance. She tried to call *The New York Times* to expose the injustice, but says she was hung up on. Next, she wrote a letter to the editor of the *New York Post.* The letter was published. One sentence jumped out: "My son is a homosexual, and I love him."

The next day, she received a phone call from Morty. "You can't believe it [the response]," he told her. "No mother has ever announced to the world her son is gay."

Through one letter, Manford and her now-deceased husband Jules were newsmakers. Together, they appeared on the Phil Donahue talk show and more than 20 different TV shows.

A 30-year veteran elementary school teacher, Jeanne Manford's activism was quite a risk at that time. "My principal warned me that there were complaints from parents," she said. "She told me to be discreet. I told her this was my private life." The principal retreated, opposition faded and Manford's life as an activist continued through her 1990 retirement from education.

What Do You Think?

Why did Jeanne Manford speak out for homosexuals? Do you think most parents would act as she did if they were in her place? Why or why not?

At the PFLAG meeting, Patsy met a woman who would change her life. Openly gay and not the least bit apologetic for it, Winnie Spellman and her partner Claudia were raising Claudia's child by an earlier marriage. Like many lesbian women, Claudia had felt societal pressure to marry a man; she had been married eight years and had a baby before she accepted that she was indeed homosexual. She spent another two years "in the closet" until she found the courage to tell her flabbergasted husband the truth.

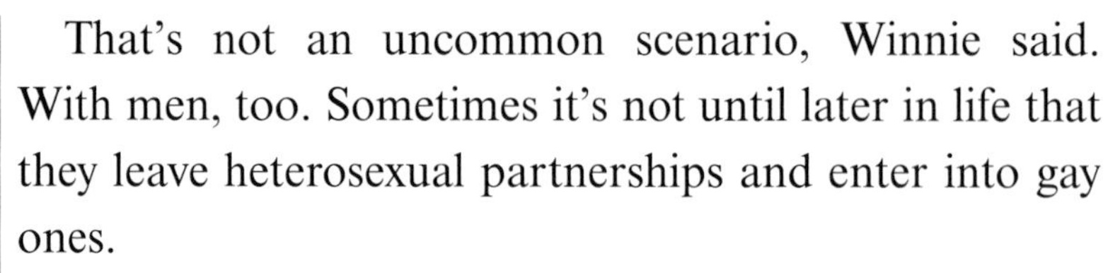

That's not an uncommon scenario, Winnie said. With men, too. Sometimes it's not until later in life that they leave heterosexual partnerships and enter into gay ones.

Heather came out when she was nineteen—coincidentally, on the same night comedienne Ellen DeGeneres did, she says with a laugh —but Patsy didn't openly discuss her orientation until she was twenty-six.

Patsy first met Heather at a bookstore, where both were browsing the green-lifestyles aisle. Heather smiled at Patsy and asked if she knew anything about hydroponic gardening. They sat down for coffee to discuss Patsy's successes and failures with tomatoes grown in that soil-free medium.

Then they met again a few days later to see a movie, then a concert, then a lecture about composting at the Cornell Cooperative Extension. Within two years they were living together, contemplating a future that, they hoped, would include children.

"I had always wanted to be a mother," Heather says. "I didn't know how it would come about, but I knew, no matter what the obstacles would be, that I wanted children."

By New York State law, they couldn't marry, and their company's heath insurance wouldn't allow either one to add on the other as a dependent. Heather's plan paid a percentage of ***in-vitro conception*** treatments, though. That, plus taking Patsy's diabetes into account, swayed them toward using Heather's body to bring new life to their family.

Their friends—gay and straight—were supportive of their decision. And once Patsy's mother realized she'd soon have a grandchild, she gave in—a little.

Since Jeanne Manford started Parents, Families and Friends of Lesbians and Gays (PFLAG) in 1972 it has grown into a national non-profit organization with over 200,000 members and supporters and over 500 affiliates in the United States.

Homosexual Parents and the Law

When same-sex couples can't marry legally, their children do not have the same legal relationship to their parents as do children of married, opposite-sex couples. Children in a same-sex household automatically have a legal relationship to their biological parent and they're eligible for the parent's health care, insurance and Social Security benefits—but children with same-sex parents have no access to the non-biological parent's benefits. Additionally if the biological mother dies, the surviving parent's custody could be challenged. The easiest way to protect the family's legal rights is to have the non-biological parent legally adopt the children. This accomplishes the following:

- An adoption not only creates a legal tie between children and their parents, reinforcing both emotional security and legal rights, it ensures that both parents are legally obligated to support the children so long as they are minors.
- In the event of either parent's death or disability while the children are minors, the children may receive Social Security and other benefits based on the deceased

or disabled parent's work record, and may also be the beneficiary of worker's compensation benefits, of a wrongful death action, and of the parent's estate. However, it is not clear how the U.S. government would respond to a Social Security claim because the United States as a nation does not recognize same-sex couples.

- Adoption means that either parent can provide employment benefits to the child, including medical, dental and life insurance. Adoption means both parents are authorized to make medical and school-related decisions. Adoption also ensures that each child may continue his or her relationship with both parents should the parents separate.

In some states, however, homosexual couples are not allowed to adopt at all, even if one parent is the biological mother. Of the states that allow gay and lesbian couples to adopt children, only New Jersey and Maine currently allow a same-sex couple to adopt in a one-step process. All other states must do so in a complex and doubly expensive two-step process. One parent first adopts and then the second can petition for joint rights.

"She doesn't accept our relationship," Patsy says. "She tolerates it."

Some people may be surprised to learn how many gay and lesbian parents there are. According to a 2007 report from The Williams Institute, an estimated two million GLB people are interested in adopting and an estimated 65,500 adopted children are living with a lesbian or gay parent.

Heather had called her parents over the years, first to invite them to a commitment ceremony she and Patsy had decided on, then to tell them about their first pregnancy. Her parents were civil on the phone, but no more. They refused to visit Heather for either the ceremony or Harrison's birth.

Although uncles and his moms' male friends surrounded Harrison, he soon figured out that he didn't have a daddy. He started asking questions when he was two, taking his moms completely off guard. But he was as excited as any child to discover he would soon have a baby sister, and he shared the news with every kid on the playground that his moms were expecting.

Heather and Patsy belong to a group of other gay parents with children, and they have learned from listening to how other parents answer their kids' questions. In the women's small community of less than 500,000, seventy families are part of the group, a number that shocks those opposed to the idea of same-sex parents and gets cheers from those in favor of the idea. The group also brings in speakers to discuss issues such as wills and other legal documents that are important for all families but especially vital for families like Heather and Patsy's.

Harrison does get some flak about his two moms, Heather says. Once kids teased him and made him cry. He came running home, full of anger and questions and confusion.

His moms patiently explained to him that not all families are alike. Some, like his friend Christopher, have two daddies, and some have only one parent, they said. "You have two parents who love you so much," they told him. "You're a lucky boy."

What Do You Think?

Do you agree that Harrison is a lucky little boy? Why or why not?

HEADLINES

(From "The Kids Are All Right," by Sadie F. Dingfelder, *APA Monitor on Psychology*, December 2005.)

An as-yet-unpublished study by Nanette Gartrell, MD, found that by age 10, about half of children with lesbian mothers have been targeted for homophobic teasing by their peers. Those children tended to report more psychological distress than those untouched by ***homophobia***.

But as a group, the children of lesbian moms are just as well adjusted as children from more traditional families, according to the data from Gartrell's National Longitudinal Lesbian Family Study. The resilience of the children may, in part, come from their parents' efforts to protect them and prepare them for facing homophobia, says Gartrell, a University of California, San Francisco, psychiatry professor.

"In order to create a homophobia-free space for these children, the moms have had to educate their pediatricians, their child-care workers," says Gartrell. "They are active in the school system and make sure there are training modules in the schools that support ***diversity*** including LGBT [lesbian, gay, bisexual and ***transgendered***] families. All this is on top of the usual 24-7 commitment to parenting."

What Do You Think?

What does this news article indicate are the advantages to being raised by lesbian parents? In your opinion do these advantages make up for the teasing you might face? Why or why not?

3 Two Fathers

"Deviants!" muttered a woman as she walked past Danny Lozniak and Lawrence Jonas. They weren't sure if she used the term because they were openly gay—or because they were walking hand in hand with their adopted son Bailey.

Terms to Understand

domestic partners: unmarried members of a homosexual couple.
solemnization ceremony: a public formal commitment celebration by a same-sex couple, similar to a marriage but without the legal recognition.
chattel: any moveable personal property, often used to refer to a slave.
unequivocal: having only one possible meaning; unmistakable.
cognitive: related to thinking, reasoning, memory, and perception.
nurturing: supportive, encouraging, promoting growth and development.

Whatever she meant, it was yet another slap in the face to two professional men who were better educated and more well-versed in culture and the arts than most of their detractors. As with any other insult that came their way, they shrugged it off—at least, on the outside. But they hate that people who didn't even know them would judge them solely on the basis of their sexual orientation (which they didn't deny but didn't flaunt, either).

Danny, a lawyer, and Lawrence, an architect, had registered as ***domestic partners*** in 2004 and then, as their commitment to each other grew, celebrated a "***solemnization ceremony***" in New

York City in November of 2005. Danny's mother had accepted Lawrence as a second son years before, and she'd watched with tears of joy as they exchanged their vows. Lawrence's family lived in Haiti and was unable to attend because of his father's health issues. Lawrence wasn't sure they would have come, in any event.

They had achieved success in their respective careers—and at forty-one, Danny was elected to the town board—before they decided they needed a child to make their life complete.

Bailey was born prematurely to a fifteen-year-old named Andrea who wanted a better life for him than she could offer. Having met Danny and Lawrence through a chain of acquaintances, she had decided when she was beginning her sixth month of pregnancy to let them adopt her baby. In the ensuing months Angela invited the men to her prenatal doctor appointments. They had hoped to make it to the delivery itself, but Angela went into labor six weeks early and barely made it to the hospital herself before the baby was born.

The latest U.S. Census statistics indicate that:

- An estimated two million gay and lesbian people are interested in adopting.
- An estimated 65,500 adopted children are living with a lesbian or gay parent.
- Gay and lesbian parents are raising 4 percent of all adopted children in the United States.

Bailey spent three weeks in the NICU—the neonatal intensive care unit—until doctors were sure his early entry into the world hadn't fated him to ongoing medical problems. On a sunny day, five-pound, four-ounce Bailey came home in the crook of Danny's hairy arm. He was soon to legally become Bailey Jonas Lozniak, the son of two proud fathers.

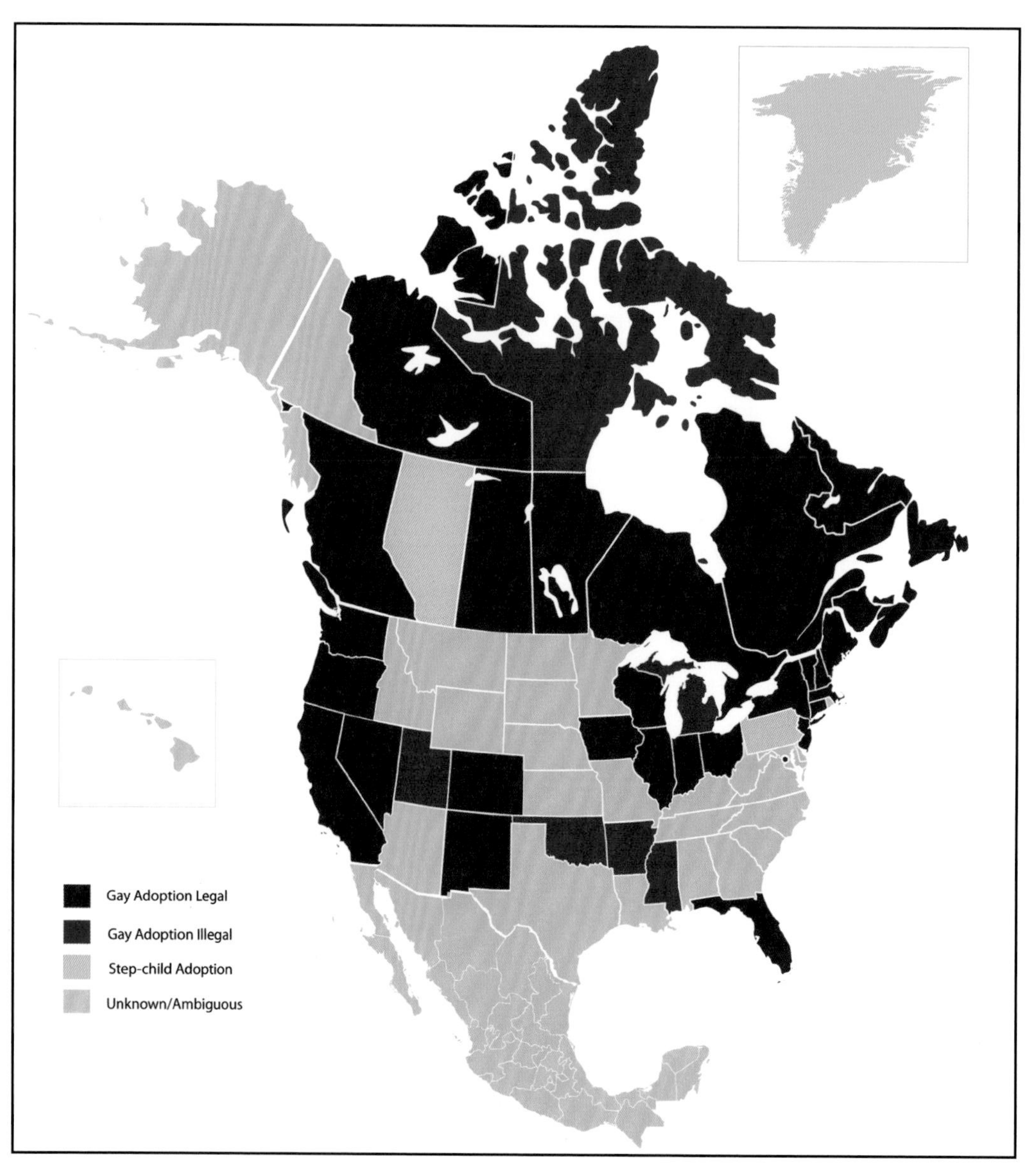

This map of North America shows the legal status of adoption by same-sex couples in the United States and Canada. Most states in the U.S. do allow a single gay or lesbian individual to petition for adoption, but laws are less clear regarding joint adoption by a same-sex couple.

Walking the baby carriage down the street, Danny wore a T-shirt stating, "I'm the dad!" Lawrence's matching T-shirt read, "And I'm the other dad!" Some strangers smiled and said, "Hey, congratulations!"

Others just scowled.

Danny had been the favorite uncle to a swarm of nieces and nephews, so unlike Lawrence, he quickly mastered the tricky maneuvers involved in warming up a bottle while holding a squalling Bailey. But Lawrence held the diaper-changing record, besting Danny by a full twenty seconds.

The two men had decided Lawrence would continue his career on a consulting basis, so he would be free to stay home with the baby. For Lawrence, life became an endless cycle of laundry, catnaps and keeping up with his architectural contract workload. Still, fatherhood was all he hoped it would be, and more—and he thought so even when walking the colicky baby in the dark of night while Danny snored on and on.

But within weeks after Bailey joined their family, Lawrence was offered a full-time position with a salary so high he couldn't turn it down. Danny was tracking his way into the highest levels of his law firm, and short-circuiting his career for daytime baby duty wasn't an option for him, either. So when he was just over three months old, Bailey joined three dozen other little ones in a local Montessori-based daycare center, where a crew of caregivers —both male and female —worked

with the even the youngest kids to fill every hour with physically and intellectually nourishing activities.

His dads were left doing the same lifestyle juggle all two-career families do: balancing housework with recreation time outdoors; doing the grocery shopping but remembering story hour on Saturday morning at the public library. On a good night, both dads tucked Bailey into bed. But even on the worst night, the dad who got home late tiptoed into Bailey's room and kissed the sleeping child on the forehead.

Danny and Lawrence were able to provide well for their son, both emotionally and financially. Nonetheless, through the years, at PTA meetings and gatherings of families, some people still looked from a distance at the two dads with undisguised disgust, and at their son with pity.

But Danny and Lawrence have hope that things are changing. After all, up until the mid-1800s in America, African-American slaves were legally-owned **chattel**; a century after that, their descendents could vote; and decades later, a black man stepped into the highest office in the United States. Only a few short years ago, mainstream America looked askance at biracial marriages (it was even illegal up until the 1960s in some parts of the country); now the fact that Danny and Lawrence are a biracial couple doesn't seem to bother people nearly as much as the fact that they're a same-sex couple! So people's attitudes do change.

Over time, public concepts of right and wrong can change drastically. This was proven in 2008 when America chose Barack Obama, an African-American man, to be the 44th president of the United States. At one time, Americans would have been shocked at the idea of a black president.

What would Bailey's life have been like if he had stayed with his family of origin? Danny sometimes wondered this as he watched their little boy move from infancy to toddlerhood. Why did people object to the idea of two parents showering love and care on a child—not to men-

tion eventual college tuition—even if those two parents were both men?

For the first ten years of Bailey's life, his fathers shielded him from any public attention. As Danny was called upon more and more to speak on behalf of civil rights—his legal specialty—he began bringing Lawrence and Bailey along and introducing them as his family. As the debate about gay rights heated up, Danny found himself increasingly becoming a spokesman for not only gays but same-sex parents.

When a local museum undertook a project showing the diversity in local immigrant and long-standing families, Danny and Lawrence were asked to be a part of the project. The two dads talked to each other, then to Bailey. Should they hold their alternative family up as an example of contemporary relationships? Some of Bailey's school friends might see photos of him and his two dads, they pointed out to him. They hadn't kept their unusual family circumstances a secret, but some people finding out about them for the first time might not understand. People might say ugly things about the two dads, they warned their son.

Bailey thought a minute, and then he stood up a bit straighter. "Then they need to learn—and we can teach them."

HEADLINES

(From "The Kids Are All Right," by Sadie F. Dingfelder, *APA Monitor on Psychology*, December 2005.)

Most of the parenting challenges Steven James, PhD, faces are pretty ordinary. For one, James's usually studious son Greg, 9, has recently been refusing to do his geography homework. "He's just not that interested in memorizing states and capitals," says James, who chairs the psychology and counseling program at Vermont's Goddard College.

However, as gay parents, James and his partner, Todd Herrmann, PhD, have some fears that don't keep most other parents up at night. The biggest one, says James, is that their sons, Greg and Max, 4, might be taken away from them if they travel to a hostile place. James and Herrmann's adoption of the two boys is not legally recognized in 11 states and many countries, and as a result they can't safely visit one set of grandparents.

"My dad and his wife were here to visit a few months ago and they asked: 'Why not bring the boys to Oklahoma?' I had to explain: 'Your laws don't respect our adoption. Your state could put the boys into foster homes without any say from me or you,'" says James.

What Do You Think?

How would it feel to be an American who wasn't comfortable traveling to certain parts of your own country for fear of losing your children? Do you think all states in the United States will eventually accept homosexual marriages and parents? Why or why not?

HEADLINES

(From "Presidential Candidate John McCain Announces Opposition to Adoption Rights for Lesbian and Gay Couples," PFLAG, July 14, 2008.)

In an interview published in Sunday's *New York Times,* Senator John McCain (R-AZ), the presumptive Republican presidential nominee, announced his *unequivocal* opposition to adoption rights for lesbian and gay couples. "I think that we've proven that both parents are important in the success of a family so, no, I don't believe in gay adoption," McCain, who with his wife Cindy is a foster parent, told the paper.

"In a country where more than 125,000 children are waiting for foster parents, Senator McCain would deny loving homes to children who desperately need them simply because of an outdated prejudice about what a family may look like," said Jody M. Huckaby, executive director of Parents, Families and Friends of Lesbians and Gays (PFLAG). "We are disappointed and saddened that a public leader who is himself an adoptive father would deny the children in America's foster care system the opportunity to thrive as part of a welcoming family. Love makes a family, but short-sighted positions like Senator McCain's can certainly tear families apart, too."

According to the American Academy of Pediatrics, "A growing body of scientific literature demonstrates that children who grow up with 1 or 2 gay and/or lesbian parents fare as well in emotional, **cognitive**, social, and sexual functioning as do children whose parents are heterosexual." The AAP has also noted that, "Overall, there are more similarities than differences in the parenting styles and attitudes of gay and non-gay" parents. Children raised by same-sex couples "seem to develop normally in every way," the group has reported.

"In fact," the Academy has said, "growing up with parents who are lesbian or gay may confer some advantages to children. They have been described as more tolerant of diversity and more **nurturing** toward younger children than children whose parents are heterosexual."

"Senator McCain's position is out of synch with the research and science and out of step with what is in the best interests of children waiting for a home and a family," Huckaby said. "PFLAG knows the pain inflicted upon families due to misinformation about [lesbian, gay, bisexual, and transgender] issues. We implore Senator McCain to take a serious look at the overwhelming evidence and listen to the stories of the countless children raised by loving lesbian and gay couples. The evidence is clear: children should not be denied access to the loving homes of gay couples."

What Do You Think?

What opinion does the author of this article hold? How can you tell? Do you agree or disagree?

4 When a Parent Comes Out

Terms to Understand

literal: following the actual meaning of a word or words, with no figurative or metaphorical language.
ordination: a ceremony at which a person takes up the full responsibilities of an official minister in the Christian church.
consenting adults: those who are of age and able to agree to take part in sexual activities.
revoke: take back; cancel.
civil unions: the legal joining of same-sex couples, providing them with rights and privileges not given to single people living together.
autonomy: independence, freedom.
validity: the degree to which something can be upheld or supported by the law.
socially sanctioned: approved or accepted by most of society.
taboo: forbidden, unacceptable, improper.

Rachel Greenleaf is proud of her parents. As a nineteen-year-old, she's not ashamed to admit that her mother and father are the two people in the world she admires most. They're both religious people, actively involved in their church's ministries, and Rachel grew up with a deep belief in God.

"They taught me that God wants my best," Rachel says. "That God wants me to live with integrity, being true to what the Bible teaches, even when that's hard to do. And I know they live what they teach, because I've seen them."

The most difficult action Rachel has seen her parents take together was the way they handled her father coming to terms with his homosexuality. "I never doubted that my mom and dad love each other," Rachel explains. "But they are both quiet people. I never saw them hugging or kissing when I was growing, the way some of my friends' parents did. I never thought much about it—but then when I was sixteen, my parents sat down with me and told me that my dad was gay. Somehow I wasn't really surprised. I was old enough that it made sense to me."

Christianity and Homosexuality

Conservative evangelical Christians (who believe that the Bible is the ***literal*** word of God) say that the Bible teaches that homosexuality is a sin. They base their beliefs about homosexuality on specific Bible verses.

More liberal Christians (including some evangelicals like Rachel and her parents) believe these verses have been misinterpreted or mistranslated. These Christians often focus instead on the New Testament messages of love and dignity for all, and use that as their basis for supporting what is sometimes known as the "gay agenda" within the church:

- protection from hate crimes based on sexual orientation
- an end to discrimination in employment and accommodation
- the right to marry or enter into civil unions
- the right to be accepted as church members
- the right to be considered for ***ordination***

Daniel Greenleaf, Rachel's father, had made the decision to move in with another man with whom he'd secretly been having a relationship for several years. "My mom had known about it for a while, but she was the only one he'd told. Even now, my mom and dad are like best friends, talking all the time on the phone even when a couple of weeks go by when they don't see each other. I think my mom misses him, and she's sad that she couldn't be what he needed. But she also really wants him to be happy. She's taught me a whole lot about what it means to love someone—I mean really love someone, the way God wants us to, not just like in the movies."

At the time, though, having her father move out to live with another man seemed weird to Rachel. "I was embarrassed to tell some of my friends," Rachel admits. "And I was mad at him too, I mean, you know, for leaving my mom and me. I thought he could have at least waited until I was out of the house. But I got over it. My dad and my mom both were good at letting me know that we're still a family, that we could still be together and have a good time, and they both still love me. After a year or so, it stopped seeming like such a big deal. I got to know Gary, my dad's partner. I can't say I exactly think of him as a second dad or a stepdad, even though he and my dad had a commitment ceremony when they started living together, but maybe that's because I'm older. He's a nice guy, though, and I can see how happy he and my dad are together."

Gay rights are very important to Rachel and her parents. They believe strongly that as people of faith they need to speak out on behalf of other gays who face discrimination, particularly in the church.

"That's what hurt us all the most," Rachel explains, "the way our church refused to accept my dad after he came out. He was the assistant pastor, and he had to resign. We knew that would happen, but we hadn't thought that people in the church would refuse to accept him even as a member of the congregation. They treated him like he'd turned into this horrible sinner. But he was the same person he'd always been, someone who prayed and read his Bible every day, someone who took his faith more seriously than anyone else I've ever known. I was so angry. I wanted to stop going to church."

But Daniel Greenleaf eventually found a church that would accept him, though he had to drive a half hour from the rural community where they lived. He went back to college and became a counselor, and eventually, he got a job working with teens dealing with gender issues. Today, Rachel and her mom attend the same inner-city church that Daniel and Gary do.

Rachel, who is majoring in theology at college, would like to be a minister someday—but she says she's worried that her own sexual orientation might get in the way. "I don't know what I am exactly when it comes to being gay or straight," she admits. "I've never had a

boyfriend—but I've never had a girlfriend either. That makes me feel a little weird, since most people who are my age all seem pretty focused on the whole pairing up thing. Right now, I just have other things to think about, I guess. But I know that eventually I want a lifetime partner. And honestly, I can imagine it being a man or a woman, so long as it's someone I truly love. I would hate to be a pastor of some church when I finally fell in love with another woman—and have to give up my career the way my father did. Besides, it just makes me so angry that my faith tradition still says that homosexuality is a sin. My mom and dad tell me that it's people like me who will be able to change things, that by people speaking up and not running away, things will

Religious denominations and churches vary widely in their treatment of homosexual members. The Metropolitan Community Church, an international fellowship of 250 Christian congregations in 23 countries, has a specific outreach to lesbian, gay, bisexual, and transgender families and communities.

change little by little. But how can I be part of something that preaches something I believe is so wrong?"

Rachel continues to struggle with her anger and hurt at a world that often doesn't accept her father's sexual orientation. "I feel confused a lot," she says. "But I'm very grateful for my dad and for my family. Maybe my life would have been easier in some ways if my father hadn't been gay—but by his coming out when he did, he forced me to think about things that are important to me now. He helped me realized what I truly value in life and what I want to do. Whether I end up being a minister—or I go to law school and become a civil rights lawyer—or I get my master's in journalism and use my writing—I know I want to do something to help change the world so that homosexuals have the same rights and respect as everyone else."

What Do You Think?

How has Rachel's life and how she thinks of herself been changed by her father being gay? In what ways do you think she would be different today if her father had never come out as a homosexual?

The Gay Rights Movement: A Timeline

1924

The Society for Human Rights in Chicago becomes the country's earliest known gay rights organization.

1948

Alfred Kinsey publishes *Sexual Behavior in the Human Male*, revealing to the public that homosexuality is far more widespread than was commonly believed.

1951

The Mattachine Society, the first national gay rights organization, is formed by Harry Hay, considered by many to be the founder of the gay rights movement.

1956

The Daughters of Bilitis, a groundbreaking national lesbian organization, is founded.

1962

Illinois becomes the first state in the U.S. to make it legal for **consenting adults** in private to engage in homosexual acts.

1969

The Stonewall riots change the gay rights movement from one limited to a small number of activists into a widespread protest for equal rights and acceptance. Patrons of a gay bar in New York's Greenwich Village, the Stonewall Inn, fight back during a police raid on June 27, sparking three days of riots.

1973

The American Psychiatric Association removes homosexuality from its official list of mental disorders.

1982

Wisconsin becomes the first state to outlaw discrimination on the basis of sexual orientation.

1993

The "Don't Ask, Don't Tell" policy is instituted for the U.S. military, permitting gays to serve in the military but banning homosexual activity. President Clinton's original intention to ***revoke*** the laws against gays in the military was met with opposition; this compromise, which has led to the discharge of thousands of men and women in the armed forces, was the result.

1996

In Romer v. Evans, the Supreme Court strikes down Colorado's Amendment 2, which denied gays and lesbians protections against discrimination, calling them "special rights." According to Justice Anthony Kennedy, "We find nothing special in the protections Amendment 2 withholds. These protections . . . constitute ordinary civil life in a free society."

2000

Vermont becomes the first state in the country to legally recognize ***civil unions*** between gay or lesbian couples. The law states that these "couples would be entitled to the same benefits, privileges, and responsibilities as spouses." It stops short of referring to same-sex unions as marriage, which the state defines as heterosexual.

2003

The U.S. Supreme Court rules in Lawrence v. Texas that laws against homosexual activity in the U.S. are unconstitutional. Justice Anthony Kennedy wrote, "Liberty presumes an ***autonomy*** of self that includes freedom of thought, belief, expression, and certain intimate conduct."

In November, the Massachusetts Supreme Judicial Court ruled that barring gays and lesbians from marrying violates the state constitution. The Massachusetts Chief Justice concluded that to "deny the protections, benefits, and obligations conferred by civil marriage" to gay couples was unconstitutional because it denied "the dignity and equality of all individuals" and made them "second-class citizens." Strong opposition followed the ruling.

2004

On May 17, same-sex marriages become legal in MA.

2005

Civil unions become legal in Connecticut in Oct. 2005.

2006

Civil unions become legal in New Jersey in December.

2007

In November, the House of Representatives approves a bill ensuring equal rights in the workplace for gay men, lesbians, and bisexuals.

2008

In February, a New York State appeals court unanimously votes that valid same-sex marriages performed in other states must be recognized by employers in New York, granting same-sex couples the same rights as other couples.

In February, the state of Oregon passes a law that allows same-sex couples to register as domestic partners allowing them some spousal rights of married couples.

On May 15, 2008, the California Supreme Court rules that same-sex couples have a constitutional right to marry. By November 3rd, more than 18,000 same-sex couples have married. On November 4th, California voters approve a ban on same-sex marriage called Proposition 8. The attorney general of California, Jerry Brown, asks the state's Supreme Court to review the constitutionality of Proposition 8. The ban throws into question the ***validity*** of the more than 18,000 marriages already performed, but Attorney General Brown reiterates in a news release that he believes the same-sex marriages performed in CA before November 4th should remain valid.

On October 10, 2008 the Supreme Court of Connecticut rules that same-sex couples have the right to marry. This makes Connecticut the second state, after Massachusetts, to legalize civil marriage for same-sex couples. The court rules that the state cannot deny gay and lesbian couples the freedom to marry under Connecticut's constitution, and that the state's civil union law does not provide same-sex couples with the same rights as heterosexual couples.

On November 4, 2008, voters in California, Arizona, and Florida approve the passage of measures that ban same-sex marriage. Arkansas passes a measure intended to bar gay men and lesbians from adopting children.

On November 12, 2008 same-sex marriages begin to be officially performed in Connecticut.

2009

On April 3, 2009, the Iowa Supreme Court unanimously rejects the state law banning same-sex marriage. Twenty-one days later, county recorders are required to issue marriage licenses to same-sex couples.

On April 7, the Vermont Legislature vote to override Gov. Jim Douglas' veto of a bill allowing gays and lesbians to marry, legalizing same-sex marriage. It is the first state to legalize gay marriage through the Legislature; the courts of the other states in which the marriage is legal–Massachusetts, Connecticut, and Iowa–gave approval.

(Adapted from www.infoplease.com/ipa/A0761909.html)

What Do You Think?

When you look at this timeline, do any of the events and their dates surprise you? Which ones? Do you think that same-sex couples should be satisfied with legal "civil unions" instead of insisting that the word "marriage" be legally applied to their relationship?

Why or why not? Do you think the legal terminology has any bearing on children of same-sex parents? Do you think homosexuality should be a legal issue—or a religious issue—or both (or neither)? Why? Does your answer become different when children are involved? Why or why not?

HEADLINES

(From "Gay Marriage Goes Way Back," by Jeanna Bryner, MSNBC, August 27, 2007, www.msnbc.msn.com/id/20464004.)

Civil unions between male couples existed around 600 years ago in medieval Europe, a historian now says.

Historical evidence, including legal documents and gravesites, can be interpreted as supporting the prevalence of homosexual relationships hundreds of years ago, said Allan Tulchin of Shippensburg University in Pennsylvania.

If accurate, the results indicate ***socially sanctioned*** same-sex unions are nothing new, nor were they ***taboo*** in the past. "Western family structures have been much more varied than many people today seem to realize," Tulchin writes in the September issue of the *Journal of Modern History*. "And Western legal systems have

in the past made provisions for a variety of household structures."

For example, he found legal contracts from late medieval France that referred to the term "affrèrement," roughly translated as brotherment. Similar contracts existed elsewhere in Mediterranean Europe, Tulchin said.

In the contract, the "brothers" pledged to live together sharing "un pain, un vin, et une bourse," (that's French for one bread, one wine and one purse). The "one purse" referred to the idea that all of the couple's goods became joint property. Like marriage contracts, the "brotherments" had to be sworn before a notary and witnesses, Tulchin explained. . . .

In cases that involved single, unrelated men, Tulchin argues, these contracts provide "considerable evidence that the affrèrés were using affrèrements to formalize same-sex loving relationships."

The author writes that "family structures have been more varied than many people today seem to realize." Does it seem likely to you, based on what you know about history and the world today? Why or why not?

Same-Sex Couples Around the World

Denmark became the first country to legalize same-sex partnerships in 1989. Within two years, Norway, Sweden, Iceland, and France followed suit. In 2001, the Netherlands became the first country legalizing same-sex marriages; Belgium followed in 2003, and Spain in 2005. The Canadian provinces of Ontario and British Columbia legalized same-sex marriage in 2003, numerous other provinces followed suit in 2004, and on June 29, 2005, the Canadian parliament passed a bill legalizing gay marriage throughout the country. On April 1, 2009, Sweden legalized same-sex marriage. Other countries offer a legal status, sometimes known as registered partnership, that confers most or all spousal rights to same-sex couples; these include Denmark, Finland, Germany, Iceland, and Norway. Countries that offer a legal status, sometimes known as unregistered cohabitation, that confers certain spousal rights to same-sex couples (and, in some of these countries, unmarried opposite-sex couples) include Brazil, Canada, Croatia, France, Hungary, Israel, New Zealand, Portugal, South Africa, Spain, Switzerland.

Find Out More

BOOKS

Bernstein, Robert A. *Families of Value: Personal Profiles of Pioneering Lesbian and Gay Parents.* New York: Marlowe & Company, 2005.

Burns, Kate, ed. *Gay and Lesbian Families.* Farmington Hills, Mich.: Greenhaven Press, 2004.

Drucker, Jane. *Lesbian and Gay Families Speak Out: Understanding the Joys and Challenges of Diverse Family Life.* Cambridge, Mass: Da Capo Press, 2001.

Garner, Abigail. *Families Like Mine: Children of Gay Parents Tell it Like it Is.* New York: Harper Paperbacks, 2005.

Gillespie, Peggy, ed. *Love Makes a Family: Portraits of Lesbian, Gay, Bisexual, and Transgender Parents and Their Families.* Amherst, Mass.: University of Massachusetts Press, 1999.

Howey, Noelle. *Out of the Ordinary: Essays on Growing Up with Gay, Lesbian, and Transgender Parents.* New York: Stonewall Inn Editions, 2000.

Johnson, Suzanne M. and Elizabeth O'Connor. *For Lesbian Parents: Your Guide to Helping Your Family Grow Up Happy, Healthy, and Proud.* New York: The Guilford Press, 2001.

Lev, Arlene Istar. *The Complete Lesbian and Gay Parenting Guide.* New York: Berkley Trade, 2004.

Snow, Judith E. *How it Feels to Have a Gay or Lesbian Parent: A Book by Kids for Kids of All Ages.* New York: Routledge, 2004.

Strah, David and Susanna Margolis. *Gay Dads: A Celebration of Fatherhood.* New York: Tarcher, 2004.

ON THE INTERNET

American Psychological Association: Lesbian and Gay Parenting
www.apa.org/pi/parent.html

Children of Gay Parents
www.childrenofgayparents.com

COLAGE: Children of Lesbians and Gays Everywhere
www.colage.org

Family Equality Council
www.familyequality.org

Families Like Mine
familieslikemine.com

Gay Parent Magazine
www.gayparentmag.com

The Gay Parenting Page
www.gayparentingpage.com

Gay Rights Watch
blog.gayrightswatch.com

National Gay and Lesbian Taskforce
www.thetaskforce.org

PFLAG: Parents, Families and Friends of Lesbians and Gays
community.pflag.org

Proud Parenting Web site
www.proudparenting.com

Bibliography

Bryner, Jeanna. "Gay Marriage Goes Way Back." MSNBC, August 27, 2007, www.msnbc.msn.com/id/20464004.

Carpenter, Mackenzie. "What Happens to Kids Raised by Gay Parents?" *Pittsburgh Post-Gazette*, June 10, 2007.

Dingfelder, Sadie F. "The Kids Are All Right." *APA Monitor on Psychology*, December 2005.

Infoplease. "The American Gay Rights Movement: A Timeline" www.infoplease.com/ipa/A0761909.html.

Owens, Tom. "One Mother's Voice: PFLAG Cofounder Recalls Group's Beginnings." Tolerance.org, July 14, 2005.

PFLAG. community.pflag.org/Page.aspx?pid=194&srcid=-2.

"Presidential Candidate John McCain Announces Opposition to Adoption Rights for Lesbian and Gay Couples," PFLAG, July 14, 2008.

Index

About the Author and the Consultant

AUTHOR

Julianna Fields is the pseudonym of a Gannett human interest columnist whose byline has also appeared in *Writer's Digest*, *American History*, *American Woodworker* and hundreds of other publications, as well as educational workbooks and a guidebook about Steamtown, a National Park Service site in Scranton, Pennsylvania. She's also a writing coach and editor.

CONSULTANT

Gallup has studied human nature and behavior for more than seventy years. Gallup's reputation for delivering relevant, timely, and visionary research on what people around the world think and feel is the cornerstone of the organization. Gallup employs many of the world's leading scientists in management, economics, psychology, and sociology, and its consultants assist leaders in identifying and monitoring behavioral economic indicators worldwide. Gallup consultants help organizations boost organic growth by increasing customer engagement and maximizing employee productivity through measurement tools, coursework, and strategic advisory services. Gallup's 2,000 professionals deliver services at client organizations, through the Web, at Gallup University's campuses, and in forty offices around the world.